DEDICATION

To my children Latiffah, Tracie-Ann and Tre'Sean, you all gave me the strength to persevere. To my better half Bo, thank you for always believing in me. To my team who kept pushing me to write. I love you and I promise to finish the very first book I started. I truly appreciate you all. Always remember, Your potential is limitless.

Copyright © 2022 Natacshia Arthur Richards
All Rights Reserved
ISBN-: 978-0-578-26530-8

No part of this publication may be reproduced, stored, or transmitted in any form or by any means, electronic, mechanical, photocopying, recording, scanning, or otherwise, except as permitted under Section 107 or 108 of the 1976 United States Copyright Act, without the prior written permission of the author. Requests to the author for permission should be addressed to the following email:

Richardsnatacshia@gmail.com

Limitation of Liability/Disclaimer of Warranty: The publisher and the author make no representations or warranties on the accuracy or completeness of the contents of this work and specifically disclaim all warranties, including without limitation warranties of fitness for particular purpose. No warranty may be created or extended by sales representatives, promoters, or written sales materials. The advice and strategies contained herein may not be suitable for every situation. This work is sold with the understanding that the publisher or the author is not engaged in rendering legal, accounting, or other professional services. If professional assistance is required, the services of a competent professional person should be sought. Neither the publisher nor the author shall be liable for damages arising therefrom. The fact that an organization or website is referred to in this work as a citation and a potential source of further information does not mean that the author or the publisher endorses the information the organization or website may provide or recommendations it may make. Further, readers should be aware that Internet Websites listed in this work may have changed or disappeared between when this work was written and when it is read.

Ordering Information: Available for quantity purchases by bookstores, wholesalers, corporations, associations, and others. For details, please visit us on the web at: *www.natacshiarichards.com*

Table of Contents

INTRODUCTION 1

DAY 1 6

DAY 2 9

DAY 3 14

DAY 4 23

DAY 5 27

DAY 6 30

DAY 7 35

DAY 8 40

DAY 9 46

DAY 10 50

DAY 11 56

DAY 12 60

DAY 13 63

DAY 14 68

DAY 15 72

DAY 16 76

DAY 17 80

DAY 18 83

DAY 19 88

DAY 20 92

DAY 21 97

DAY 22 102

DAY 23 107

DAY 24 110

DAY 25 115

DAY 26 120

DAY 26 124

DAY 27 129

DAY 28 135

DAY 29 140

DAY 30 144

ABOUT THE AUTHOR 149

LIFE QUESTIONS

1. WHAT IF ASKED WOULD OTHERS SAY ABOUT YOU?
2. WHAT DO OTHERS USUALLY SEEK YOUR ADVICE FOR?
3. WHAT ARE YOUR TOP 3 PERSONAL DEVELOPMENT BOOKS?
4. WHAT IS YOUR GREATEST ACHIEVEMENT?
5. WHO ARE YOUR 3 TOP MOTIVATIONAL SPEAKERS?
6. WHAT IS YOUR PURPOSE IN LIFE? WHY?
7. WHERE DO YOU SEE YOURSELF IN THE NEXT 3 YEARS?
8. WHAT MAKES YOU HAPPY?
9. WHAT ARE YOUR STRENGTHS?
10. WHAT ARE YOUR WEAKNESSES?
11. DESCRIBE YOURSELF IN 5 WORDS?
12. HOW DO YOU THINK OTHERS PERCEIVE YOU?
13. DO YOU PRACTICE EMOTIONAL INTELLIGENCE?
14. WHAT HAVE YOU DONE FOR YOU LATELY?
15. DO YOU PRACTICE SELF-LOVE?
16. WHEN DID YOU LAST LAUGH SO HARD IT HURT?
17. WHAT'S YOUR #1 PRIORITY?

18. DO YOU HAVE A FORGIVING HURT?
19. ARE YOU A STARTER OR A FINISHER?
20. ARE THERE ANY ANSWERS YOUR SEEKING ABOUT YOUR LIFE?
21. WOULD YOU LOVE TO SPEND QUALITY TIME WITH YOURSELF?
22. DO YOU HOLD YOURSELF ACCOUNTABLE FOR YOUR OWN ACTIONS?
23. WHAT LIFE LEGACY ARE YOU LEAVING BEHIND?
24. WOULD YOU WANT YOUR SON OR YOUR DAUGHTER MARRY SOMEONE LIKE YOU?
25. DO YOU STAND FOR WHAT YOU BELIEVE IN OR ARE YOU A PEOPLE PLEASER?

"Success isn't about how much money you make, It's about the difference you make in people's lives"

— Michelle Obama

Introduction

$\mathcal{A}$re you tired of being tired? I pray as you read this book it assists you and facilitates your breakthrough. We all go through challenges in life that may leave us stuck. I wrote this book to encourage and inspire others to start their journey to self-improvement. Are you ready to take that **JUMP?** Are you ready for that **SHIFT?** Well for me, I decided never to be stuck again. So, I had to figure out a way that will pull me out of the pit of extreme depression. Yes, you read that correctly. I suffer from depression, anxiety, and PTSD. I fight everyday to stay positive and I wish to spread that positivity with you all. This book will help you to manifest anything you want out of life. I made a pact with myself to not allow my past to determine my future and not allow my current situation be my final destination. A wise man once said, that your condition is not your conclusion. There are affirmations in this book that will move you. Each word, each line, each sentence, has been curated to kick-start your path towards manifestation. We all need to start from somewhere and I want this to be your start. Manifest improvements into your relationships, career, finances, education, love life, spirituality and every other part that's of importance to you. In case you didn't know, it takes just 21 days to cultivate a habit. But here I am, giving you 30 days. 30 days of injecting absolutely nothing but positivity into your life. Then, you'll begin to realize how it's going to impose change and revert every negativity. Words have power and the tongue is the source of that power. Therefore, you must be careful how you use them. You have the power to bless or curse with the words that come out of your mouth. You can choose to use them constructively or destructively. We must always learn to align our words with our thoughts. Words and thoughts are a powerful, life transformative duo that is highly underestimated. I truly believe that if you speak life to yourself daily, you will be able to rewire your brain to think more positive thoughts. I've experienced elevation throughout my life. I've also experienced failure, and hurt. I've been in my own way for a long time. Do you have the courage to start the journey of setting yourself free? It's time to break the chains that's been holding you back. Those chains are inclusive of generational curses, low self-esteem, failed relationships, abuse, weight loss, weight gain, mental illness, and the list goes on. In 30 days, this book will transform you both emotionally and mentally. Get your pen and paper ready. Ready Set Go!

"Strength does not come from what you can do. It comes from doing the things you thought you could not do."

— Unknown

"Don't allow the process to punk you out of YOUR spot."

— Natacshia Arthur Richards

I AM

ENOUGH!

DAY 1

Being enough doesn't mean being perfect. Being enough is about celebrating your imperfections. The mistakes you make in life are acceptable because it's inevitable. No one is perfect so the idea of perfectionism can be thrown out the window. When a person aims for perfection, endless frustration is the end result. When you say **I am enough**, you are saying you're not done growing because growth is a continuous cycle. It doesn't stop. In today's society, we are made to think that we are not enough and it's all based on what we wear, the amount of likes and following we have on social media and even the type of car that we drive. When you look around and notice you don't "fit" into the societal standards set by fellow human beings, you begin to criticize yourself. Even when you do your best and you tell yourself that it's not enough. Stop right now, go and look in the mirror. You are unique. You are more than good enough and there is no other person like you. We allow the stress from the outside world to make us think otherwise. Although we are our worst critics, we don't always have to listen to it. You need to shut down the whispers the moment negative thoughts come to mind. I allowed those negative thoughts to hold me back for years but I started to condition my mind and shifted it into the right direction. Listen up! you are enough and you need to hold your head high so you can walk in your purpose.

THINGS TO TELL YOURSELF WHEN THINKING YOUR NOT GOOD ENOUGH

- ❖ THIS WILL MAKE ME STRONGER
- ❖ THIS TOO SHALL PASS
- ❖ MY FAILURES ARE LESSONS
- ❖ YOU HAVE SO MUCH TO BE THANKFUL FOR
- ❖ YOU DON'T NEED THEIR APPROVAL TO BE GREAT
- ❖ YOU ARE NOT WHERE YOU STARTED
- ❖ FOCUS ON THE PROCESS NOT ON PERFECTION
- ❖ YOU CAN'T HATE YOUR WAY INTO LOVING YOURSELF.

I CHOOSE

ME!

DAY 2

You have made the conscious decision to make YOU a priority. We often hold on tightly to the things that will not take us to the next level. Let go of all that baggage because it will continue to drain you. If it's not helping you to elevate, then it's time to let go. I believe in the law of attraction. The more you start removing things, habits or people that are not serving your life's purpose, you will make room and attract the people and things that align with you and your purpose. When you choose yourself you will not be disappointed. Choosing yourself means you have decided to focus on your happiness and deflect all the negativity that comes your way. This is the only way to reach your goals in a positive way. You'll stop thinking about what others think or say about you. You must decide to always love yourself through the good and the bad times. There have been many cases where we place other people's needs above ours. I think it's about time you choose you, or you will be forced to deal with the consequences of **NOT** choosing yourself as life goes on. Stop allowing people to disrespect you. Stop allowing others to abuse you mentally, physically or emotionally. The fear of embarrassment and loneliness has confined you to relationships that should have been over years ago. It's time to choose you and value your time. Remember, your time is extremely valuable and there are other productive things you can spend your time on. Though you can use your time to make money, you can't use money to purchase more time. We all have the same 24 hours in a day. You have to be willing to say, as valuable as I am, so is my time and I need to put myself first. It's one of your most valuable assets that you should give away willingly. Choosing you does not mean that you can't depend on others, it means you will ease the pain from the possible disappointment you may end up enduring in the process of relying on others. Each passing day, when you stand up for yourself you learn to respect yourself more. This right here is known as a self esteem builder. Check out a few of my top picks for choosing you.

"If You Don't Do The Choosing Life Will Do It For You"

— Natacshia Arthur Richards

"You Have The Power To Choose The Life You Want To Live"

— Natacshia Arthur Richards

TIPS ON CHOOSING YOURSELF

- ❖ Establish your expectations.

- ❖ Acknowledge your own emotions.

- ❖ Decide what you are willing to tolerate

- ❖ Make yourself a priority

- ❖ You must learn the art of saying NO!

- ❖ Stop caring about what others think about you

- ❖ Live in your truth

- ❖ Hold yourself accountable

- ❖ Know the power of NO!

- ❖ Fall in love with yourself unconditionally.

I LET GO OF WHAT I CAN'T CONTROL

DAY 3

That quote has the prayer of serenity written all over it. Why hold on to things you can't control? **LET IT ALL GO!** This doesn't mean life has to stop. It means you are no longer accepting the things you can not control. You are getting behind the driver's seat and you're taking control of your life. You're accepting of the stage you currently are in life by allowing yourself to live through the wave of positive energy. This way you don't have to lose peace and become troubled with the ups and downs from the adventurous roller coaster we call life. Most of us don't want to let go of things we like or love because we're too comfortable. We don't realize that when we keep our claws attached to these habits or people, it does more harm than good. It can wreck our lives in the long run. For example, staying in a relationship where you're constantly being disrespected. You stay because a part of you keeps hoping that there's a possibility for this person to change but later you're filled with disappointment because they never do. There isn't anything you haven't done. You've given them the best years of your life and one day you wake up 18 years later and you realize that you should have left a long time ago but you're now 18 years older. Some people start to feel hopeless and become depressed because they think they've missed out on love and no one else would want them as they are. Broken. To be free, you must learn to let go. Then, you must dig deep to find out what is making you hold on so tightly. Why are you ok with being disrespected? Do you think you deserve it? Today's society teaches us that we should endure everything even if it kills us on the inside because we look good together physically. There's no care for the mental and emotional part of the relationship but as long as we look good, that's all that matters right? Wrong. A lot of times the crippling factor that causes the resistance to leave is **fear.** Fear of losing the false identity we believe to be us because it's wrapped up into the things we refuse to let go of. Who were you before these things, behaviors or the relationship? The fear of the unknown scares us. Fear is an illusion and it only appears to be real if we believe them. It was once said that our limitation is only an imagination. I get it, letting go is not an easy thing to do. But if you don't get to the core of why you can't let go, you will continue to live with the same behaviors and ruin your relationships. Romantic and platonic. I do need you to know that letting go is not as hard as you think ethier. You must have discipline so you can get through it. With discipline, determination, and consistency it can be accomplished.

God Grant Me The Serenity To Accept The Things I Can't Change, The Courage To Change The Things I Can And The Wisdom To Know The Difference

— Reinhold Niebohr

TIPS FOR LEARNING HOW TO LET GO

- ❖ MAKE THE DECISION TO LET GO
- ❖ MAKE PERSONALIZED AFFIRMATIONS
- ❖ MEDITATION
- ❖ YOU HAVE TO TRULY BELIEVE AND HAVE FAITH YOU WILL BE OK.
- ❖ YOUR GOAL IS TO BE FREE. FREEING YOURSELF OF ATTACHMENT TO PEOPLE AND THINGS.

THINK BACK TO TIME IN YOUR LIFE WHEN YOU KNEW IT WAS TIME FOR YOU TO LET GO. HOW LONG DID IT TAKE YOU AND WHAT WERE THE STEPS YOU TOOK TO GET THERE?

_____
_____
_____

Moment of Truth

BEFORE DOING ANYTHING, ASK YOURSELF THESE QUESTIONS.

WHAT IS IT THAT YOU WANT FROM WHATEVER IT IS YOUR DOING RIGHT NOW.

_____

_____

WHY DO YOU WANT IT?

_____

_____

WHO BENEFITS FROM THIS GOAL?

_____

_____

WHAT ARE YOU WILLING TO GIVE UP TO GET IT? ie, laziness, procrastination, and comfort zones. These are sacrifices.

_____

_____

WHO WILL YOU BECOME AFTER ALL OF THIS IS ACCOMPLISHED?

_____

_____

HOW DO YOU FEEL RIGHT NOW KNOWING YOU CAN MANIFEST ANYTHING YOUR HEART DESIRES?

_____

_____

"Man Is Made And Unmade By Himself.
In The Armory Of Thought He Forges The
Weapons Which Will Destroy Him. He Also
Creates The Tools With Which He Will
Build For Himself Heavenly Mansions Of
Joy And Strength. Between These Two
Extremes Are All The Grades Of Character,
And Man Is Their Maker And
Their Master"

— James Allen

I AM

HUMBLE

Have you learned anything new about yourself through the first few chapters?

_____
_____
_____
_____
_____
_____
_____
_____
_____
_____
_____
_____
_____
_____
_____
_____
_____
_____

"Whatever The Mind Of Man Conceive
And Believe, It Can Achieve."

— Napoleon Hill

DAY 4

When we research the definition of humility, we find out that it's a modest view of one's importance. Some people may look at being humble as a sign of weakness. But it's **not**! A person who lacks humility is arrogant and there have been traces of narcissism found in these kinds of people. Being humble means you are wise enough to know you are not better than others. You're able to admit when you're wrong and you know when to ask others for forgiveness. Humble people tend to handle stress a lot better, they know how to ask for help when it's needed and are grateful for what they have. Humility is the foundation for growth. It helps you to open up to people by unlocking the door to give them a glimpse at your imperfections and that builds trust between you and that person so he or she can reciprocate that openness with you. People admire others because of their modesty and integrity. Humility also allows you to be meek. When you are willing to learn from others, gaining wisdom is endless.

ATTRIBUTES OF A HUMBLE PERSON

- ❖ SPEND TIME LISTENING TO OTHERS.
- ❖ PRACTICE MINDFULNESS
- ❖ SEEK FEEDBACK FROM OTHERS
- ❖ THE TAKE TIME TO SAY THANK YOU
- ❖ THEY ASK FOR HELP
- ❖ THEY ASSUME RESPONSIBILITY

QUESTIONS

HOW DO YOU DEFINE HUMILITY?
_____
_____
_____

WHY IS IT IMPORTANT TO BE HUMBLE?
_____
_____
_____

IS THERE DANGER IN BEING TOO HUMBLE?
_____
_____
_____

WHAT ARE EXAMPLES OF HUMILITY?
_____
_____
_____

WHAT IS YOUR EVALUATION OF YOUR LIFE LIVING?
_____
_____
_____

I AM CREATING WHAT I WANT TO BE

DAY 5

You and I have the power to turn our desires into reality. First you must envision yourself at the level you aspire to be in life. Financially, physically, spiritually, and mentally. You have to speak these things into existence but first, what are you doing to condition your mind for your future? If you want it bad enough, it can and will be yours. I always say that you need to walk and talk as if it's already yours. For instance, you can write a check to your future self in the amount you will be cashing in because you believe that later on you will be capable of affording it. That is the practicality side of manifestation. The more you see it, the more you're going to continue working towards it. Look beyond where you are. Your thoughts, your words and your actions must come into alignment. Start by saying, I have decided to engage in a vision bigger than myself and get up every morning to speak this to yourself in front of the mirror. After, recite affirmations to recharge your worth, your confidence and your mind. You can create your own affirmations that will mirror your future self that you've envisioned. Just remember, your past should never define your future. What are you waiting for?

A Few Affirmations to Work With

- ❖ I AM FEARLESS
- ❖ I INSPIRE OTHERS
- ❖ NO ONE CAN MAKE ME FEEL INFERIOR
- ❖ I HAVE THE COURAGE TO SAY NO
- ❖ I HAVE THE POWER TO CHANGE MY STORY
- ❖ I WAS NOT MADE TO GIVE UP ON MYSELF
- ❖ I USE MY FAILURES AS MY STEPPING STONE
- ❖ I CHOOSE ME EVEN IF OTHERS DON'T
- ❖ OTHERS DON'T DEFINE WHO I AM
- ❖ EVERYTHING THAT I TOUCH TURNS TO GOLD

I AM

WEALTHY

DAY 6

When I speak of wealth, I am not only referring to financial wealth. Others have an interesting definition of what wealth means to them. It could mean being able to provide for themselves and their loved ones, having a big house, the flashiest car, the largest collection of jewelry and so on. As Gucci mane said "you get the bag and fumble it, I get the bag and flip it and tumble it." We all want bags of wealth at the tip of our fingers but how can we access it? This chapter helps us to start the process of **goal digging.** We set up our goals, learn the necessary information, apply it, plan the execution and go out there to flip and tumble our investments so we can bring home that bag. Man, it is sweet when we can taste the sweetness of victory once we accomplish that goal. But, let's talk about other types of wealth. Wealthy to me also means being rich in faith itself. Not everyone believes in the same belief as I do. That is why I won't turn this into a sermon but to me, faith is an amazing gift. I used to walk by sight alone until I had undergone many life challenges. Gradually, my faith that was as small as a mustard seed began to grow. I basked in the richness that faith had to offer. I understood that I could not question why all those things happened to me when I saw that I walked through the burning fire and came out on the other side unburnt. Though I felt the scorching flames, it didn't show. When you see me, I don't look like what I went through. It is God who graced my life with His presence and enlightened my understanding. He brought me to this point that I am now and has made me knowledgeable of His truth. I have become patient and prayerful because I know that whatever is for me will be for me and no one can take that away. I am also rich in love. Love is abundant in my life. I experience love with my family and friends who are not ashamed to profess their love for me. They don't only say it but they prove it. I would be lying if I said I never experienced love. I am rich in love with being able to travel, love for my pets, love for my passions such as writing impactful books like these that will change the world. My passions also involve helping others by motivating and inspiring them. Love is the fuel that drives my life. Yes, money is very important. That is non debatable and we are reminded of this on a daily basis when those bills start to roll in. It can be incredibly overwhelming the bills signify our priorities. So instead of just attaching money to the definition of wealth, let's rephrase it and define it by using the following words. **Love, family, faith, freedom, helping others, making an impact**. I had to grow into the person that has the ability to get the bag. I had to have the qualities that allowed me to do so.

QUESTIONS

What does the word *WEALTH* mean to you?
_____
_____
_____
_____

If you had a chance to ask one of the wealthiest people a question, what would it be?
_____
_____
_____
_____

Do you have specific written goals?
_____
_____
_____
_____

What are the most important things to you in life?
_____
_____
_____
_____

How do you measure life?
___
___
___
___

What do we need most in this world?
___
___
___
___

What makes you special?
___
___
___
___

What do you think your purpose is?
___
___
___
___

What are their primary needs and concerns in life?
___
___
___
___

I AM

POSITIVE

DAY 7

"Tell Me How You Use Your Spare Time, And How You Spend Your Money, And I Will Tell You Where And What You Will Be In Ten Years From Now"

— Napoleon Hill

"A Positive Mine Finds A Way It Can Be Done; A Negative Mind Looks For All The Ways It Can't Be Done"

— Napoleon Hill

When you remain positive, you are hopeful. It's being able to see your glass half full instead of it being half empty. It's about optimism and always spotting the rainbow after a storm. I started conditioning my mind to find the good in the bad. A few words associated with positivity are **courage, certainty** and **self-esteem**. This does not mean you have an understanding that obstacles are inevitable. It means you're not giving negativity the upper hand to rule your life. When you condition your mind it directly affects your thoughts and if your thoughts are positive, then you will be able to push forward in life without dwelling on the past. No regrets. You focus more on the solution and less on the problem. Staying positive allows you to heal faster if you're sick. Stress can negatively affect your recovery but positivity can aid in your coping and stress management skills. With positivity as your backbone, you will be able to approach your challenging situations strategically. Based on what you believe in, you can start your day with prayer, words of affirmation and meditation. Positivity is infectious and once you bask in its glory, others will partake in it as well.

BENEFITS OF THINKING POSITIVELY

- ❖ LONGER LIFE SPAN
- ❖ BETTER STRESS MANAGEMENT
- ❖ BETTER COPING SKILLS
- ❖ LENGTHENS THE TIME OF RECOVERY LOWER DEPRESSION AND ANXIETY
- ❖ BETTER PSYCHOLOGICAL AND PHYSICAL WELL BEING
- ❖ CULTIVATE A POSITIVE ENVIRONMENT ADD VALUE TO SOMEONE ELSE LIFE
- ❖ IDENTIFY YOUR AREAS OF NEGATIVITY AND PRACTICE GRATITUDE

SURROUND YOURSELF WITH POSITIVE PEOPLE

WHAT ARE SOME OF THE WAYS YOU REMAIN POSITIVE WHEN FAST WITH PROBLEMS?

_____
_____
_____

THINK OF A SITUATION YOU WHERE IN AND YOU DIDN'T HANDLE IT WELL. WHAT COULD YOU DO DIFFERENTLY?
_____
_____
_____

WHAT ARE YOU GRATEFUL FOR AND POSITIVE ABOUT RIGHT NOW?
_____
_____
_____

WHAT IS ONE PROBLEM YOU'RE THANKFUL YOU DON'T HAVE?
_____
_____
_____

WHAT ARE YOU GREAT AT?
_____
_____
_____

WHAT GET YOU EXCITED ABOUT LIFE?
_____
_____
_____

I AM GOD'S MASTERPIECE

DAY 8

Some may say, they don't feel or look like a masterpiece. Stop allowing the poison called negativity to occupy your mind. God created us in His own image and likeness so therefore you are God's masterpiece. I used to struggle thinking I wasn't good enough. That feeling of worthlessness. I didn't feel pretty enough and I wasn't small enough so I was always trying to figure out ways I can make myself better. I went from working out 7 days a week to working in the operating rooms handing the doctor the surgical instruments while completing a tummy tuck to later be the one to be laying on the table to have a procedure of my own. I wear many hats and one of them is being a surgical technologist. I was one of the first classes to graduate from LIU as a surgical tech. I was able to work closely with doctors and from there, I began to brainstorm different ideas for the type of work I can do to enhance my beauty so that I could look like a masterpiece. When that wasn't good enough, I resorted to breast implants which I thought would do the trick but it was too big and I had to go back to have them removed. The doctor said that the size of my butt was big enough and I didn't need fat transfer. But I disagreed with his advice and decided that it should be used as fillers for any cellulite that was visible back there. The fat melted away but my cellulite remained. I can laugh about the experience now that I can reflect on it without regrets. Although I am on my weightloss journey, I refuse to beat myself up about it and I am moving to the beat of my own drum. I am getting out of my own way. I was never the type of person to care about other people's opinions. What I cared about the most was mine. It took time, several turns and hurt but now I can stand tall today and shout it from the mountain top and proudly say that I am **God's masterpiece**. We are not masterpieces because of our appearance. The grace of God is the reason we wear the masterpiece badge. No matter what you've been through or going through, your masterpiece status remains untouched. We are all a working process but God's grace keeps us covered while we continue our healing journey. We all hold a special place in God's heart but in His eyes, we are a priceless work of art handpicked by Him alone.

"We Find Out Who We Are When We Lose The Things That We Used To Define Us"

— Unknown

QUESTIONS

HOW DO YOU DEFINE BEAUTY?
_____
_____
_____
_____

WHO ARE YOU?
_____
_____
_____
_____

IF YOU MULTIPLY RIGHT NOW, WHAT TYPE OF WORLD WOULD WE BE LIVING IN?
_____
_____
_____
_____

WOULD YOUR EXISTENCE MAKE A DIFFERENCE?
_____
_____
_____
_____

I AM

COURAGEOUS

DAY 9

With great power comes great responsibility. Being courageous does not mean you walk into the room with a louder speaker, announcing how courageous you are. Being courageous means that if you fall, you can get back up and try again. It doesn't matter how many times you fail, you think about how you can succeed on your next try. It takes courage to be successful. It takes courage to be a fighter. Every step we take in life, is taken out of courage. Two captains can not be on one boat that is why fear and courage can not coexist in one's life. You have to choose which one you will let override your mind and your goals. Some people find it difficult to develop the courage they need. They are frightened by their challenges but courageous people look their challenges in the eye. But the good news is that it's never too late to live a courageous life. Courage helps you to graduate from follower to leader. It wipes out the presence of fear. Keep in mind that no one was born courageous. It's a virtue we develop overtime and helps us to give the best of our abilities. Don't live your life stuck in a traffic line. Let courage fly you high, push you forward to boldly take risks and equip you with strength when you feel weak.

WAYS TO LIVE A MORE COURAGEOUS LIFE

- ❖ IF YOU FACE YOUR FEAR YOU WILL HAVE BE ABLE TO LEARN HOW TO OVERCOME IT.
- ❖ BY FACING YOUR FEAR YOU CAN IDENTIFY YOUR STRENGTHS
- ❖ YOU CAN PRACTICE STEPPING OUT OF YOUR COMFORT ZONE.
- ❖ THINK POSITIVELY
- ❖ ACCEPT YOUR CHALLENGES

The Mission Statement

IT IS MY MISSION TO INSPIRE YOU SO YOU CAN INSPIRE OTHERS AND MAKE A SIGNIFICANT IMPACT IN THEIR LIVES. TO ALWAYS TREAT OTHERS WITH RESPECT LOVE AND KINDNESS WHILE REMAINING HUMBLE. TO LIVE LIFE WITH INTEGRITY AND EMPATHY. NEVER FORGETTING CONSISTENCY, DISCIPLINE AND DETERMINATION IS FOLLOWED BY SUCCESS.

I AM GRATEFUL

DAY 10

The word gratitude comes from the latin word **gratus**, which means pleasing or thankful. Living with gratitude is fundamental for your well being, your relationships and your health. Appreciation softens us. When you form the habit to be grateful, it's easier to see what you have instead of complaining of what you don't have. You feel much better about yourself when you're grateful. A person who is grateful does not feel like the world owes them anything. The more grateful you are, the more blessings, opportunities and favors you receive. You jump those hurdles with ease and the doors that have been locked will open. Gratitude allows you to improve and promote better social behavior. Gratitude starts small. Be grateful for the air you breathe, for wisdom to live your life, the food on your table, your functioning body parts, the job you have, your family and friends, the roof over your head and your pet if you have one. These are things that money can not buy. Gratitude doesn't take anything out of it. Instead, it puts peace and insight into you. What you need to do is take a second everyday to think about all the things you're thankful for. You may not be where you want to be but the truth is, you're not where you used to be. If you're not grateful, you live a life of complaining, misery and anger. IT becomes unbearable to be around you and people will slowly distance themselves from you. Grab a pen and paper and jot down what you're grateful for.

QUESTIONS

What are you most grateful for?
_____
_____
_____

What have others done for you that you're grateful for?
_____
_____
_____

Who has helped you become the person you are today?
_____
_____
_____

What's the best thing that has happened to you today so far?
_____
_____
_____

Have you received any blessings that you least expected?
_____
_____
_____

QUESTIONS

Who in your life survived something difficult and how do you feel when you think about the fact that they're still here?
___
___
___

What act of kindness did you do today?
___
___
___

What did you read or listen to today that added value to your life?
___
___
___

When was the last time you felt loved?
___
___
___

What is one positive thing you can say about yourself?
___
___
___

QUESTIONS

What have you stopped doing that you're grateful for?
_____
_____
_____

What hard lessons are you grateful for?
_____
_____
_____

What past or present relationships are you grateful for?
_____
_____
_____

Can you think of any non-physical gifts your greatful for?
_____
_____
_____

What have you learned about yourself that will help you in the future?
_____
_____
_____

I AM

BLESSED

"When Some Things Go Wrong, Take A Moment To Be Thankful For The Many Things That Are Going Right"

— Unknown

DAY 11

God bestows His blessings upon us even when we don't think we're deserving of it. As we are unique individuals, I know that the meaning of being blessed may vary for some of us. A set of people may feel that they are blessed because of the materialistic things in their possession. Being blessed doesn't revolve around the kind of car or how many friends you have. If something was to happen to you this very second, you would leave these material things behind. When I look to my left and to my right, I am blessed to see the sun rise, I am blessed to have life, good health and strength to carry out my daily tasks. We only say we're blessed when things are going smoothly. Have you ever thought to yourself that you're still blessed even in the midst of adversity? When you fall ill? When money is scarce? On the verge of eviction? Are you only blessed when life is going right for you the way you want it to? I am blessed with a forgiving heart. A lot of people associate being blessed when the circumstances are only in their favor. I believe 2020 is a memorable year for everyone. In that same year, I was plagued with several medical issues: stroke, congestive heart failure, weak muscles in my legs, which resulted in me having to rely on a can for mobility. Prior to falling ill, I never thought I would have to use an albuterol pump but now, after going through all of this I still feel blessed. Regardless of what I'm going through right now, I am aware that I am still blessed. I am blessed because I made it through. I am blessed because

I know that people who may have gone through what I did, may not have been lucky enough to still be standing. You have to look at the bigger picture when you answer the question: are you blessed? I am blessed because my spiritual blessings are superior to any earthly blessing I may have. I am blessed because of God's forgiveness and how He redeemed me through his blood.

QUESTIONS

What do you think it means to be blessed?
_____
_____
_____

What are some of the blessings you received last year?
_____
_____
_____

Write down a list of blessings you received, materialistic, non materialistic things. Think of one way you can bless someone this week with one of those same blessings?
_____
_____
_____

Can you embrace the good and let go of the bad?
_____
_____
_____

Can you find one reason to be happy?
_____
_____
_____

I CONTROL

MY

THOUGHTS

DAY 12

When you are able to control your thoughts, you can influence your lifestyle. Your life reflects your thoughts and your thoughts reflect your life. You are the pilot of your life and that makes you in charge of your outlook in life and your outlook determines your happiness. Rome was not built in a day and with that understanding, it will take time to master the art of controlling your thoughts. Meditation is a great tool to start with when you want to control your mind. When practiced consistently, it enhances both cognitive and psychological behavior. It requires silence, extreme focus and open-mindness. I've transitioned to the world of meditation as well and so far it has helped me maintain my sanity, have inner peace that has shown on the outside by reducing stress and helping me to focus on my priorities. You can't meditate in a rowdy environment that's why you must wait until you're comfortable to get it right. Start with 5-10 minutes a day. That's all it takes. Just five minutes to breathe and relax. Gradually, you can extend the time when your schedule is less hectic. There are different methods of meditation. Whether you're engaging in it for spiritual enlightenment, fasting or to reduce stress, it's important to pick the right method that is best for you.

"Growth And Development Requires Healing"

— Natacshia Arthur Richards

I AM

A MONEY

MAGNET

DAY 13

When you think about the power behind attracting money, you must first think about how much faith you have in attracting it. Do you believe it? Do you truly believe you're a money magnet? What are your thoughts on prosperity? Do you know about the **laws of attraction?** The energy you put out into the universe is what you will get in return. You must be submissive to change. Doing a complete 360 to your mindset so you can manifest the things you want. It's about being in alignment. You must appreciate the money you have in order to receive more of it. Don't pay attention to the amount. Big or small, you should not shove it carelessly in your side pocket of your favorite mom jeans or the darkest part of your wallet. I was once the kind of person that would stuff my money inside the tiny pocket attached to my bag. The little details matter in everything you do. If you can not respect, organize, and take proper care of your money, how will you be able to handle larger amounts when they come? Organize your money properly so you can attract more of it. Buy a calendar and highlight your payment dates on it, build or repair your credit, and avoid unnecessary spending. This shows seriousness. It also shows wisdom in being financially responsible. The goal is to continue being a money magnet. Speak over your money. When I'm making use of my money, I like to say **"more money."** This increases my faith that one day there will be an abundance of money. How will it happen? The truth is, I don't know but I believe it will. I also believe that you are a money magnet. So, speak it into existence. Remember that Benjamin Franklin once said that if you fail to plan, you plan to fail. Pay your bills on time, monitor your bank account, save, and invest.

"Too many people spend money they haven't earned to buy the things they don't want, to impress people that they don't like"

— Will Rogers

STEPS TO TRANSFORM INTO A MONEY MAGNET

- ❖ ELEVATE YOUR BELIEFS ABOUT MONEY
- ❖ CHANGE YOUR MINDSET
- ❖ SPEAK YOUR MONEY ATTRACTING AFFIRMATIONS WHILE BEING SPECIFIC
- ❖ PRACTICE GRATITUDE FOR THE MONEY YOU ALREADY POSSESS

EXAMPLE:

"I AM FINANCIALLY ABUNDANT

I RELEASE ALL RESISTANCE TO ATTRACTING MONEY

MONEY FLOWS FREELY AND EFFECTIVELY TO ME.

I AM WORTHY OF RECEIVING MONEY IN EXCHANGE FOR MY SKILLS

I AM CONNECTED TO A SUPPLY OF DEPOSITS, OF CONSTANT CONTINUATION OF FUNDS IN MY ACCOUNTS"

I BRING JOY

TO OTHERS

DAY 14

How much does it cost to spread joy to others? Not one dime. The power to spread joy to another human being is priceless. It improves your lifestyle while impacting the people around you. I love making others smile. Showing some token of appreciation or just even being kind and helping those who can't help themselves, thrills my heart. This will make you more attractive and you will exude positivity. When joy overtakes your life, it elevates your health and you become worry free. Your ability to push through difficulties in life will make you an exemplary choice to people in need of inspiration. Being an inspiration to others brings them joy because it gives them hope. When you compliment others, when you show concern, when you pay attention and show compassion, all of these can brighten up another person's day. It starts from our homes and to the strangers we encounter during the day. Negativity is a choice and so is feeling joyful. Joy is a feeling that emanates from our being. Here are a few tips on how to cloak yourself with joy while changing one life at a time. No one wants to be around someone who oozes negativity. I challenge you to smile and spread love daily. Your smile is medicinal. That one simple act can heal a broken soul.

"The Greatest Gift You Can Give To Others
Is The Gift Of Unconditional Love
And Acceptance"

— Brian Tracy

TIPS FOR ARMING YOURSELF WITH JOY WHILE SHOWERING OTHERS WITH IT

- ❖ SMILING AT PEOPLE YOU SEE
- ❖ DO SOMETHING YOU LOVE
- ❖ SPEND TIME WITH YOUR LOVE ONES
- ❖ ENCOURAGE OTHERS
- ❖ VOLUNTEER YOUR TIME
- ❖ DONATE TO CHARITY

I AM

KIND

DAY 15

Being kind will help you build a village of like-minded people. Kindness boosts up your immune system and our body's natural oxytocin levels. Do you know the same oxytocin also expands blood vessels and that reduces blood pressure? This should sway your heart to become kind. But it's beyond the personal benefits. It's a high moral standard that everyone should exhibit. We should always strive to do the right thing. We are certain of the influence kind words could have on someone but there's usually a resistance. This occurs because of past experiences and the hurt of it not being reciprocated. Which is completely normal, but you shouldn't cut your blessings because of another person. You shouldn't be kind because you expect anything in return. Let kindness flow through you naturally with any expectations. Don't give, to get. The difference between someone who is kind naturally versus someone who is acting like they are, is that, when they don't receive any incentives, or blessings in return, it doesn't change them. You can only pretend for so long. Eventually, your true nature comes to the surface. Being kind is also apologizing if you've offended someone. By doing this you're helping yourself to become a better person. Kindness helps us to forgive. It's fixated on generosity, sympathy, and empathy. What you live behind, will speak for you forever. Be kind to yourself and be kind to others.

QUESTIONS

How would you describe a kind person?
_____
_____
_____

Why is it important to be kind?
_____
_____
_____

How can you be kind to others?
_____
_____
_____

What was the last act of kinded you completed?
_____
_____
_____

Consider kindness before you speak
_____
_____
_____

QUESTIONS

Don't discriminate who to be kind to.
_____
_____
_____

Practice good intentions
_____
_____
_____

Reach out to others. even if they don't
_____
_____
_____

Be kind everyday
_____
_____
_____

Thank someone who you appreciate
_____
_____
_____

I LEARN

FROM MY

MISTAKES

DAY 16

Learning from your mistakes is accepting what has transpired and being able to move on from it. You teach yourself to avoid repeating that same mistake. We're human and no one is above mistakes. Once you put your lessons into action it turns into growth. Your mindset plays a major role in how you view your mistakes. When you make peace with your mistakes, you approach situations differently. It allows you to reevaluate and recreate your goals. When you make a mistake, you shouldn't beat yourself up over it. You need to strengthen your mind so you can turn your mistake into a lesson. Self-awareness gives you the opportunity to reflect, so you retrace your steps and understand why you made that mistake. It doesn't erase the past, but it opens the door to a wiser future. Life is a journey and when you hurry to seek perfection, you make more mistakes. Which many at times can be irreversible. Acknowledge your mistakes, feel the pain, deal with the repercussions, and heal. But how can you analyze your mistakes? Let me help you out with that.

HOW TO ANALYZE YOUR MISTAKES

- ❖ ASK, WHAT WENT WRONG
- ❖ WHAT I DO WRONG
- ❖ HOW DO I FIX IT
- ❖ IDENTIFY THE SKILLS, RESOURCES, TOOLS AND KNOWLEDGE THAT WILL KEEP YOU FROM REPEATING THE MISTAKE.

THINK BACK TO A TIME YOU MADE A MISTAKE YOU DIDN'T THINK YOU COULD GET OVER

- ❖ What did you learn from it?
- ❖ How did you improve?
- ❖ What steps did you take to ensure it doesn't happen again?
- ❖ Teach someone else this technique so it will not happen to them.

"The best way to predict the future is to create it."

— Peter Drucker

I AM
A GOD/
GODDESS

DAY 17

A God and a Goddess with no principles to live by have no integrity. They are bursting with high positive energy, passion, and authenticity. They have qualities that everyone can easily gravitate to. A Goddess has unshakable confidence, and she knows that there is more to her than her physical beauty. She is a woman of virtue and noble character. She is kind, humble and disciplined. Her diligence can include preparing nutritious food for her family, displaying selflessness by sacrificing her needs. She is wise beyond her years and her loyalty knows no bounds. A God has the power to do anything he sets his mind on. He is disciplined and consistent, he is the head and never the tail. But the head cannot function without the legs. A God will walk hand in hand with his Goddess and always place her on the highest pedestal. He is one of a kind just like her. That is what makes their pairing unique. Words cannot captivate who he truly is. He is the epitome of love and is loved by many. Along with a powerful Goddess beside him, the sky is his limit. Now, go and walk in your godly purpose.

"A True Hero Isn't Measured By The Size Of His Strength, But By The Strength Of His Heart"

— Hercules

MY PAST DOESN'T DETERMINE MY FUTURE

DAY 18

We all have things in our past we conquered to get to where we are now. Past mistakes and traumatic experiences have somehow snuck their way into our lives. Some of us are still reliving the nightmare and are fighting through the aftermath daily. Let me quickly narrate a story about a little girl who endured internal scares and became a conqueror. Her upbringing was rough, and it was worse living with an extremely abusive mother. A mother who would turn on the stove and have the little girl's hand hovering above the fire. At the young age of 8, the girl was committed to a psychiatric ward because she was "acting out." Not realizing that the bad parenting skills was the reason for her misbehavior or should I, **acting out**. What kind of parent would do something like that to a child that she birthed? This little girl grew up with the belief that her mom hated her. Was it because of the uncanny resemblance between the little girl and her father? Who knows? The little girl happened to be the middle child out of five children. It came to a point where she couldn't bear the beatings anymore. After two failed attempts to run away, her plan finally worked. She broke out of the place she dreaded the most and she didn't care where she would end up. She just wanted to get as far away as possible. Later, she was placed in foster care but the treatment she received in the first two homes were terrible. They say the third time's a charm, right? Unfortunately, life is not a fairytale. When she found herself in the third foster home, it was like jumping from frying pan to fire. The abuse worsened physically, and emotionally. The system she relied on, failed her. The family she was placed with appeared to be loving but looks like they say can be deceiving. Shortly after her arrival, her foster father began to molest her. There was no one there for her and she had no one to confide in. The only way to express herself was to **act out.** One day, she pulled out a knife on her foster brother and immediately, she was taken out of the home. As you can see, there's a pattern. Lack of concern and abuse contributed to her pain and her behavior, but no one saw the signs. Instead, they labeled her as the problem. There wasn't any effort to inquire what really happened in that home for her to do what she did. Actions are triggered by another action. Fast forward to this girl's adult life, she has grown up to become an advocate for many. She conquered. This story could have ended differently. I am not saying she did not go through any issues because of this, but what I am saying is that your past should be your drive. Let it charge you up and catapult you to the place you want to be in the future. The place you can't stop dreaming about. It all starts with you. It starts with how you conquer your battles. That little girl went to college, earned her bachelor's and her master's degree because she had to realize that she was solely in charge of her life. She wrote a new chapter after closing out the old ones. That little girl is me.

"Every Adversity, Every Failure And Every Heartache Carries With It The Seed Of An Equivalent Or Greater Benefit"

— Napoleon Hill

"The Ultimate Measure Of A Man Is Not Where He Stands In Moments Of Comfort And Convenience, But Where He Stands At Times Of Challenges And Controversy"

— Martin Luther King Jr

I AM STRONGER THAN MY EXCUSES

DAY 19

You can either fight for your dreams or let your excuses win. Usually, people fight hard to come up with excuses and I used to be one of them. Have you put on your armor and marched out into the battlefield to fight for your dreams? or have you been enabling your excuses to stop you from reaching it? Excuses are destiny killers. You need to drop every excuse you came up with because it's destroying you. There are many factors in life that hold us back and one of them is living a life filled with excuses. Whenever we come across the slightest discomfort, we find an excuse to not continue. When we want to start a new project, either online, business, education, or fitness, we make up excuses to not start. We say things such as: I don't have the time, I'm too busy (everyone's favorite line.) The reality is everybody is busy. Adulthood doesn't get any easier. You must make time for the things that matter and the things that will change your life for good. If you wish to go back to school, it is never too late. If you've let yourself go and you know you need to get back into the gym, it is not too late. You can do it. Your color, your size, your height, your sexual orientation isn't a hindrance when it comes to living in your truth. There is no excuse to not be successful. There is no excuse to not be healthy, there is no excuse. Where there's a will, there's a way. It's all about determination. Stop self-sabotage and replace it with self-discipline. The beauty about life is that we can learn and unlearn. Self-discipline can be learned and self-sabotage can be unlearned. There's a new version of you waiting right outside that door of lame excuses.

"Challenges Make You Discover Things About Yourself That You Never Really Knew"

— Cicely Tyson

I WILL MASTER MY OWN EMOTIONS

DAY 20

Wise and successful people are in control of their emotions. A lot of us have allowed our emotions to form a life of its own. The saying goes "he who angers you, conquers you." In simpler words, when a person has the power to anger us or sadden us, it means we have lost control of our emotions. It is your responsibility to not let anger or sadness consume you. In my life journey so far, I refuse to have anyone other than myself control my emotions. Believe me when I say that I have failed at this repeatedly. This is not an easy trait to acquire, but I will not give up until I fully tap into it. You become more powerful when you are in control of your emotions. You become dangerous to others who are frustrated with their own lives and are looking for people to project that frustration on. To be in control, you must know your triggers. Your triggers are your red flags, something that easily irritates you and could make you lash out. When people lash out, they've lost control. A captain without control of his own ship, will sink. And the passengers on board will sink right with him. The passengers represent the people in your life. When you can't control yourself, the people around you suffer. They would have to tread lightly so they don't set you off. But you can't live like that. You need to alleviate yourself from any relationship, friendship, workplace, or even place of worship, that will cause you to get out of character. When you don't react, it infuriates the oppressor because they know it's going to be hard to bring you down. This advice isn't telling you to not express yourself, it's telling you to not overexpress. Once you speak your mind, do not dwell on the negativity because then it will make you prone to excessive anger or sadness. This is an emotional and psychological game changer that will put you at the top.

"You Have To Train Yourself To Be Stronger Than Your Emotions Or Else You'll Lose Yourself Every Time"

— Unknown

Tips on Mastering Your Emotions

- ❖ KEEP TRACK OF POSITIVE EXPERIENCES
- ❖ GAIN NEW CONCEPT
- ❖ DISTINGUISH YOUR EMOTIONS MORE
- ❖ WHAT MESSAGE IS YOUR EMOTIONS TELLING YOU
- ❖ BECOME CONFIDENT
- ❖ TAKE ACTION
- ❖ USE HEALTHY COPING STRATEGIES
- ❖ BRAINSTORM SOLUTIONS
- ❖ CHANGE PERSPECTIVES
- ❖ IDENTIFY WHAT YOUR FEELING

I AM

WORTH IT

DAY 21

What would you rate your self-worth? There are people who believe they are worthless. They believe their worth is defined by the materialistic things they lack, their level of education, economic status, or physical appearance. This will make you understand that despite your achievements, you are still worthy. Worth equates to value and when people think they are not valuable is because they don't have self-worth. We are living in a microwave society whereas we all want results instantaneously. Life is a process so if you want results, you should think long term. But before you can think long term, you must think the journey is worth it. You must think you're worth it. Do you think you're worth it? If you answered yes, then how come your belief about yourself isn't reflecting in the things you lay your hands to do? Every morning, you go to your 9-5 and you know deep down you would like to establish your own business. Why don't you take the risk and invest in yourself? You have bright ideas that could change so much in the industry you plan on going into but because you don't know your worth, those ideas are just sitting there going to waste. Every drop of blood, sweat and tears that goes into the necessary steps is worth it because you're worth it. But to know your worth, you must ask yourself why. Why do you want to make changes to your life? Once you know your why, your purpose is clearly defined and it is easier to perform the right way in the right direction. You will then feel the need to surround yourself with individuals whose goals are in alignment with yours. It may not mean you have the same exact plan, but the commonality is your sense of worth and your passion to achieve the goals you have written down. I have people like that in my life and I chose one of them to become my accountability partner. No one is an island and when the road gets a little tough, it goes a long way knowing there is someone who can see and feel you slipping, they can help you get back on track. Let's get you started. Here are a few steps in building a better you.

SELF-WORTH TIPS

- Know your worth
- Get an accountability partner
- Set daily goals
- Get up and start again
- Know your strengths and interests
- Learn from your mistakes
- Make sure you're giving yourself enough time to complete tasks. Don't rush.
- Get rid of anything that doesn't add value to your life
- Focus, Focus. Focus
- Respect the process

SELF DISCIPLINE QUOTES

"Beautiful gems can emerge from dirt.
struggle can teach you self-discipline and resilience."
— **Dipa Sanatani**

"The pain of self-discipline will never
be as great as the pain of regret."
— **Unknown**

"Success doesn't just happen, You have to be intentional
about it, and that takes discipline."
— **John C.Maxwell**

"The price of excellence is discipline.
The cost of mediocrity is disappointment."
— **William Arthur Ward**

"Self-discipline begins with the mastery of your thoughts.
If you don't control what you think, you can't control what you
do. Simply, self-discipline enables you to think first
and act afterward."

— **Napoleon Hill**

I AM

CONFIDENT

DAY 22

Confidence isn't about feeling superior to others. It's your inner knowledge. It's being sure of yourself and trusting in your abilities. The most powerful person in a room is not usually the loudest. It's the person who can command a room with silence. How you walk into a room is part of that judgment. As you walk in, give direct eye contact and walk with your head held high and with your shoulders pushed back. This will make you look like you're in command. But it isn't only about looking like you're in command. You must feel like you are. We've all struggled with confidence in our lives at some point. In our appearance, relationship, decisions making, and careers. Lack of confidence has kept many people from moving forward in life. Which is why you have to believe in yourself and anything you lay your hands on. If you're lacking confidence you must first find out the cause and in what area you lack it. And when you do, you must think about how to not only improve but how to increase it. Think back to the last you felt the most confident. What empowered you to feel that way? Remember there is only one you and that's what makes you unique. So step out of your comfort zone and go after the goals you want to accomplish. As you grow your skills in the area you lack confidence, your confidence as a whole will grow. Physical appearance is one of the most popular areas in which people lack confidence. Feeling beautiful is being comfortable in your own skin. There's no definition because words can't describe it.

It's a feeling. You can put on makeup, throw on 5 inch heels and look hot but it's isn't just about feeling and looking good about yourself outwardly. But inwardly too. Your personality should and must match. A person that is considered beautiful is categorized as so not only because of their beauty but because they're kind, humble and have integrity. Their inner beauty shines so brightly that you can't help but to want to be around them. Beauty is being able to empower yourself and others. It's being confident. Take the time to get to know yourself more. Loving yourself more makes you see the beauty that you exude and it boosts your confidence. Fall in love with the person you are now, so you can become the best version of yourself. Beauty is the soul's expression. Beauty is a mindset. Our society is so focused on the physical things and it has left so many women questioning whether they are beautiful or not. Are they too big or too small, short or tall. Are their teeth straight enough? If you ever find yourself struggling with any of these, get up, go and look into the mirror and list three features you love about yourself. Then, look past any and all imperfections and remember that despite what others may think about you, you are beautiful.

Questions to ask yourself while on the journey of building your confidence.

What area do you lack confidence in?
_____
_____
_____
_____

Where would you like to have more confidence?
_____
_____
_____
_____

When do you feel self doubt?
_____
_____
_____
_____

What makes you unique?
_____
_____
_____
_____

Questions to Ask Yourself While on the Journey of Building Your Confidence.

List three things you did today that went well.

_____
_____
_____
_____
_____

The first step toward developing lasting self-confidence is to practice acceptance of your strengths and your challenges. List your greatest strengths and why you're grateful for them. List your three greatest challenges and what you can learn from them.

_____
_____
_____
_____
_____
_____
_____
_____
_____
_____

I BELIEVE

IN ME

DAY 23

Self-esteem lays the foundation for self-belief. Believing in yourself equates to having faith. You must have faith in your capabilities and know when it's time to give yourself credit, when credit is due. Some of us cannot celebrate our small wins because of low self-esteem. We feel like we didn't do our best and there is nothing worth celebrating. The secret to your success lies in your belief. How strong is your belief? Have you ever thought about how much believing in yourself makes a difference in your quality of life? Once you think you can't do something your mind absorbs that thought and mentally stops you from doing it. You've already put out the negativity in the air stopping your growth. You must believe in yourself to move forward. The fear of failing stops a lot of people. You should never fear failure. How will you know your strength or weakness in a particular area if you don't try? Fear is an illusion. It's false evidence appearing realistic. Stop allowing it to stunt your growth. You missed opportunities along the way because of it. Failing at something is really the best teacher. You already know what you did wrong. You can do it by applying all the things you've learned when you failed the first time. Start by setting small goals. Goals are definitely needed, you need to have an idea of your final destination. Treating yourself with a nurturing nature is an important aspect of developing belief in yourself. You will be able to teach others to believe in you also. You first have to show them that your belief level in yourself is 100% This may not be as easy as reading it this. Do know, you are resilient so should you happen to fall, get back up and keep going.

I LOVE ME UNCONDITIO NALLY

DAY 24

When you love yourself you accept yourself for exactly who you are. The good, the bad, the ugly, the flaws, and everything that comes with you. You realize that you're a full package right? And just like any package that lands on your doorstep, you are responsible for it. In this case, you are responsible for learning how to manage and regulate your own feelings. It also means you need to take care of your well being by eating healthy, drinking plenty of water and getting enough sleep. When you love yourself you define your own worth. You don't need validation from others. You experience self love when you're giving of yourself. And you should not allow anyone to use or take advantage of you either. True love is loving ourselves not judging ourselves. Loving yourself flaws and all. The goal is to live our best life with no regrets. Loving you with no strings attached is showing yourself unconditional love. Once you can show yourself unconditional love you can love others the same way as well. Stop waiting for others to love you how you want to be loved. Loving yourself and putting yourself first comes from a deep gratitude. Be grateful for who you are, how you look and how far you've come. This is a struggle for many due to their insecurities. They worry about what others say about them and always compare themselves to others. You will never achieve loving yourself unconditionally if you can't face your insecurities. I need you to realize that you have what it takes to accomplish loving yourself unconditionally. Treat yourself like the queen that you are. Accept the things you can't change. Practice gratitude, and start living a healthier life by eating healthy. Start treating your body right. Drink plenty of water and accept that some people will never like you. Those are not your people. After embracing your flaws there is nothing no one else can say to make you feel less than a queen. It is never too late to become the man or woman that you are destined to become. This is the start of your journey. If you happen to stumble along the way get back up, hold your head up high and keep going. Remember what I said in chapter 23. Walk into every room like you own it. You're in total command. The world is waiting for the new you.

SELF-LOVE TIPS

- START EACH DAY WITH POSITIVE AFFIRMATIONS
- EAT HEALTHY, HYDRATE AND EXERCISE
- SURROUND YOURSELF WITH POSITIVE PEOPLE
- DON'T COMPARE YOURSELF TO OTHERS
- STAY AWAY FROM TOXIC PEOPLE
- LOVE YOUR DIFFERENCES
- DON'T WORRY ABOUT OTHERS OPINIONS
- YOU WILL MAKE MISTAKES BECAUSE YOU ARE NOT PERFECT
- UNDERSTAND WHAT YOU FEAR AND WORK ON IT
- FEAR IS FALSE EVIDENCE APPEARING REAL

"You yourself, as much as anybody in the entire universe, deserve your love and affection"

— Buddha

"We just need to be kinder to ourselves. If we treated ourselves the way we treat our best friend, can you imagine how much better off we would be?"

— Meghan Markle

"In order to love who you are, embrace the experiences that shaped you"

— Alexis Maria Caceres

I AM

FREE

DAY 25

Being free is generally having the ability to act or change without restraints. It's being free of wasted time, addictions, abuse, self-pity, not living the life you desired. It's breaking free of the chains that's holding you back. Chains of depression, toxic people, anxiety, your past, insecurities, your faults, failed relationships and anger. I truly believe freedom also look different for everyone. Freedom is conquering anything you may be battling and accept your struggles. Freedom is fearing nothing. Working for yourself and traveling the world. Freedom is your continued growth and not allowing anyone around you to stop it. Freedom is loving yourself even if no one does. It's not feeling guilty for being true to yourself. Freedom is making your own choices and accepting the bad things that may have happened to you. They can't be erased but you will not allow it to stop you from experiencing self-love. Freedom is loving yourself with no end. Stop putting chains back on God allowing you to break free from. Doesn't the idea of freedom appeal to you? Don't you want to break free from the negative patterns that've been in your family for years? Those patterns that have become a part of your history and are now limiting you from succeeding? I'm talking about the things that's constantly being repeated. You know the saying that goes. "History repeats itself." Only thing is now it's not just a quote but it's become your life. We don't have to keep repeating them. Although these curses have an effect on our current lives we have the choice to put a stop to it or continue in the footsteps of our ancestors. When we continue we then pass the curses down to our children. Then from them to your grandchildren. The pattern never stops until you break the chain. Patterns have many consequences. You must recognize the destructive behavior and put a stop to it. Change the course of the road you must go down, take another road so you can have a better outcome. Let's break the change NOW!

" *If you practice the principles you can participate in the promise*"

— Stormy Wellington

"*Freedom is loving yourself to the core. Flaws and all*"

— Natacshia Arthur Richards

HABITS TO HELP YOU PROSPER

- ❖ NET WORK
- ❖ DREAM BIG
- ❖ STAY FOCUSED
- ❖ GET UP EARLY
- ❖ INVEST IN YOURSELF
- ❖ READ MORE BOOKS
- ❖ STEADY PERSONAL DEVELOPMENT
- ❖ DON'T ALLOW OTHERS TO WASTE YOUR TIME
- ❖ TAKE CALCULATED RISKS
- ❖ WRITE DOWN YOUR GOALS
- ❖ MAKE YOUR HEALTH A PRIORITY
- ❖ LEARN FROM PEOPLE YOU ADMIRE
- ❖ FOSTER MEANINGFUL RELATIONSHIPS
- ❖ CULTIVATE AN ATTITUDE OF GRATITUDE
- ❖ TAKE ACTION
- ❖ MAKE YOUR WHY POWERFUL

I FEAR

NOTHING

DAY 26

Fear is often described as False Evidence Appearing Real. Although fear is a natural response to physical danger, we can also be the ones creating it ourselves. Fear has been in existence for years and when we were kids, we got a taste of it. We were scared of the boogie man, the dark, clowns, cats and heights. But when we grow up, some of these fears may remain and new fears settle in. Some people refuse to love others because of the fear of rejection. That kind of fear creates paranoia, anxiety and worry. Three things that we don't need in this already complicated world. We have a better chance of overcoming fear by facing it head on. Some things we fear are not actually dangerous. For example, public speaking is something I feared all of my life. I had to overcome this. I needed to be able to speak to others about my business and mental health awareness. I couldn't do that with fear hanging over my head. Some people fear skiing and have never gone skiing before. They may never go but they will go on a ski trip. This is fearing the unknown. Educate yourself about the facts and risks you face when doing the things you fear. Face them and learn about them. Keep a journal, practice mindfulness and keep calm doing it. You will overcome your fears and anxiety. Stay the course and you will conquer your fears and release yourself from being held hostage from them.

TIPS TO OVERCOME FEAR

- ❖ TAKE SMALL STEPS
- ❖ KEEP MOVING DON'T STOP
- ❖ BREATH THROUGH PANIC
- ❖ DON'T TRY TO BE PERFECT
- ❖ FACE YOUR FEARS AND LEARN ABOUT THEM
- ❖ APPRECIATE YOUR COURAGE

"Don't Allow The Fear Of Falling, Hold You Back From Living A Life With No Regrets"

— Natacshia Arthur Richards

I AM UNSTOPPAB LE BABY

DAY 26

When you feel unstoppable, you feel like you can climb the highest mountain. You've developed mental toughness to handle any adversities. So before we continue, I would like to congratulate you for building self-control, self-discipline, self-confidence, and determination to win. Unstoppable people are categorized as warriors. They are ready to conquer the world. They have a light inside of them that never goes out. They remain in their own world competing only with who they were the day before. They don't allow the negative voices of others to get into their head, whispering things that counter their positive spirit.. Even if it's an impossible task, they want to show the world that there is no such thing as impossible. They set goals, write out plans and execute them. Unstoppable people keep their dreams alive until it becomes their reality. They develop the necessary skills to make it happen and never second guess themselves. They could care less if others do not see the vision they have for themselves. If they screw up, they start all over again. Even though it's tough. But that's why they're warriors. They fight. They will keep their eye on the goal, throw away the failed plans and create a new one. Don't try to get in the way of an unstoppable person because they end up proving to you that any dream (not just theirs) is achievable. You need to hang around unstoppable people. Their spirit and their mindset is courageous. They will never stop trying to be a better version of themselves. Unstoppable people say things like, "Help me", "How can I do it?", "Give me a second chance", "I took your advice", "I can do it." Unstoppable people are also champions. After fighting, they conquer and when the battle is over, they're the champions. They have all it takes. Hello, my name is Natacshia and I'm unstoppable. No one or nothing will ever get in my way. I walk in victory even if I fall.

TO-DO LIST

- ❖ Don't be afraid of the consequences of failure.
- ❖ Don't ever compare yourself to others.
- ❖ You are limitless potential
- ❖ Change what you can
- ❖ Be fully committed.
- ❖ Have humility and apologize when your wrong
- ❖ Stay true to yourself
- ❖ Always be in control
- ❖ Have no fear
- ❖ Discover your purpose

"There is a powerful driving force inside every human being that, once unleashed, can make any vision, dream, or desire a reality."

— Tony Robbins

"If you can dream it, you can do it."

— Walt Disney

I'M A

GOAL

DIGGER

DAY 27

Almost got you there didn't I? In this instance, the gold you need to get is your goal. A Goal Digger is a woman or a man who seeks ways in bettering themselves. They're very ambitious and have goals. But what makes them stand out even more, is their unstoppable spirit. We call that "resilience." They surround themselves with success by working day and night until they create the life they want to live. There is nothing more sexy and attractive than someone who is a hustler and sets goals. Not only do they set it, but he or she crushes every last one of them. A goal digger likes to surround themselves with like-minded people. They believe the company they keep should be able to inspire and or motivate them. Goal diggers are always trying to improve. They never compete with others and they don't worry about their position on the ladder of success compared to others. Although it is said in the book of Matthew that "all you need is faith as small as a mustard seed," goal diggers also put in the work to get what they want. Remember, "faith without work is dead." I've always been a driven self-motivated person. Now am I motivated every single day? Of course not. That's unrealistic. However, I do surround myself with people who motivate me. I also listen to sermons and motivational speakers daily and most importantly, I celebrate my small wins. I go back to look at my why while embracing my mistakes. Then, I continue to push forward. Now, ask yourself this. Are your goals smart?

Specific- exact nature of your goal

Measurable- how will you track your growth?

Attainable - is it realistic?

Relevant- how is this goal applicable to your life and future?

Time-bound- when is the deadline for achieving this goal?

HABITS FOR GOAL DIGGING

- ❖ ESTABLISH GOALS/ SELF REALISTIC GOALS
- ❖ MAKE SURE YOUR GOALS ARE A PART OF YOUR PLAN
- ❖ PRIORITIZE
- ❖ DON'T COMPETE WITH OTHERS
- ❖ BE ACCOUNTABLE
- ❖ BE DETAILED
- ❖ TRUST YOURSELF
- ❖ ARE YOU A GOAL DIGGER
- ❖ WHAT IS YOUR MOTIVATION FOR CREATING GOALS
- ❖ WHAT ARE THE FIVE MOST IMPORTANT VALUES IN LIFE RIGHT NOW?

"Dream Enormously Big,
And Celebrate Small Wins"

— Natacshia Arthur Richards

"If You Really Want To Do Something, You Will Find A Way. If You Don't, You'll Find An Excuse."

— Jim Rohn

I AM THE HEAD AND NOT THE TAIL

And The Lord Will Make You The Head And Not The Tail; You Shall Be Above Only, And Not Be Beneath...

— Deuteronomy 28:13

DAY 28

WHEN YOU ARE MADE THE HEAD, YOU ARE ON TOP OF YOUR circumstances. As the head you are the leader and decide the direction your life will be going. ALTHOUGH YOU WILL GO THROUGH LIFE EXPERIENCING PROBLEMS AND ADVERSITIES, YOU CHOOSE TO BE ON TOP. YOU DON'T ALLOW YOUR FALLS TO DEFINE YOU, YOU get up and keep it moving. This builds character and makes you a stronger person. While remaining at the top you live out your principles and values. You are a product of your decisions and you've decided to stay on top no matter how many times you have to get back up. Always remember, that your character is the foundation your results will be built on.

"God Didn't Create Us To Be Average.
We Were Created To Excel."

— Ephesians 1:4

"I Am In A Constant State Of Attracting All The Good That I Deserve And I Desire."

FORGIVENESS

DAY 29

I decided to forgive myself as well as others. I forgive myself for settling for less than I deserve as well as the past. I forgive myself for failed relationships, for my weakness, for those I've judged. For my lost dreams, self- sabotaging and moments of laziness. I forgive myself for not practicing what I preached. Forgiveness is very important for the healing process. We hold on to anger, shame, resentment and sadness. We get stuck because we refuse to forgive. Forgiveness gives you freedom, freedom; freedom from being captive to all resentments. I can't forgive half way, It's all or nothing at all. Stop punishing yourself and others for past mistakes. Don't you want peace? I did, I had to learn to forgive a mother I felt hated me from birth. Stop punishing yourself, let go and embrace your peace. Some will never apologize to you, and it's ok. Your soul deserves peace. Open up room for your blessings. Forgiveness is not for the weak. Being able to forgive those who've done you harm takes strength, faith and understanding. I'm talking about strength on a spiritual level. Your soul needs peace, learn to let it go. You may never understand why others did the things that they did. Sometimes it's a struggle but hate the sin not the sinner. Forgiveness is for your own growth and happiness. I truly understand how you might be going through it right now. It's a tug of war trying to forgive at times. Some people may never be able to forgive and the offense has affected their mental state. If it gets to the point where nothing is working for you to get through the tough times, and you need help coping. Once you don't have the ability to forgive on your own. Seek professional help.

"Forgiveness Does Not Mean You Forget, It Means You Begin To Heal."

— Tre'Sean Calique Richards

"In Order To Forgive Others, You Must Know To Forgive Yourself."

— Tracie-Ann Joy Richards

SELF-SABOTAGING

DAY 30

Self sabotaging is when you actively or passively take steps to prevent yourselves from reaching your goals .It's behaviors such as procrastination, self medication with alcohol, eating disorders, and many more are the most common. You do these things because you lack self-worth and don't believe in yourselves. If you continue to tell yourselves that you're not good enough, then that is what you will always believe. As human beings, we believe the truth we tell ourselves and sometimes that truth can be a lie. You would then lack confidence to be the best you can be. Your fear of success stops you from becoming successful. To become fearless of success, you must first define your own meaning of success.

> "As A Man Thinks, So Is He."
> — **Proverbs 23:7**

You start telling yourselves all kind of negativity. Such as, Well I'm not going to pass that test anyway. Once you etched that in your heads you forfeit all positive thoughts; allowing you to study for this exam.

Steps to Stop Self-Sabotaging Behavior

- ❖ Change patterns of behavior
- ❖ Set goals and write your plan out
- ❖ Stay positive
- ❖ Speak life into your life
- ❖ Understanding and identifying triggers
- ❖ Having self compassion
- ❖ Anticipate and plan for obstacles
- ❖ Seek professional help if you need to
- ❖ There is no shame in needing help
- ❖ Find a therapist

BREAKING GENERATIONAL CURSES

CONGRATULATIONS

YOU'VE COMPLETED 30 DAYS OF BECOMING A BETTER VERSION OF YOURSELF. YOU HAVE LEARNED SEVERAL THINGS ABOUT YOURSELF IN THESE LAST 30 DAYS AND IT'S NOW TIME TO PUT IT ALL TO TEST. IT TIME TO PUT YOUR LESSONS INTO MOTION SO YOU CAN MANIFEST ALL OF YOUR HEART DESIRES. DON'T FORGET TO HOLD YOURSELF ACCOUNTABLE FOR YOUR ACTIONS. THAT INCLUDES THE ONES YOU DO INTENTIONALLY AND UNINTENTIONALLY.

READY, SET, GO!

LIFE IS LIKE RIDING A BICYCLE.

TO KEEP YOUR BALANCE,
YOU MUST KEEP MOVING.

ABOUT THE AUTHOR

Natacshia Arthur Richards is the mother of three beautiful children 32, 17, and 15. Grandmother to three little princesses and the granddaughter to the Reverend Wilma Brown. Known to wear many "hats" Natacshia is an International mental health advocate and a serial Entrepreneur. Having the first-hand experience of needing assistance from others, life for her began as a child in the foster care system during the 80s. She resided at the Wading River Institution before transforming her pain into purpose. Natacshia has a Master's Degree in Healthcare Administration and started working for the NYS Office For People With Developmental Disabilities in 1996, where she helped people with developmental disabilities live richer lives. She also worked for a private agency in 1995 and thereafter, began building a platform on social media for the sole purpose of spreading mental health awareness and suicide prevention. That platform is known today as, "You Have a Purpose". It has since reached people in over 5 countries and various states such as Antigua, the UK, Philippines, Slovakia, Canada, and the US. With a burning love for giving back to the community Natacshia, has fed the homeless for over 15 years, contributed to coats and clothing drives, collected and participated in the toy drive at Woodhull Hospital for children and families affected and infected by the Aids virus during the holiday season where she dressed as Mrs. Clause.

Her life's mission is "To inspire others to dig deep within to identify and fulfill their life's purpose. Encouraging them to find Hope and Strength from those who were unable to accomplish their own dreams. Reminding them to allow that forgotten goal, your parents, grandparents or children to motivate you to push even harder and to never permit a lack of effort to be the cause of murdered dreams". That right there should be reason enough for anyone to try again. Find the beauty in attempting again, this time around you already know your previous mistakes, giving you the upper hand. Always remember, your L's (losses) are actual lessons. As humans, Respect, Love, Kindness and Humility are key attributes we all should strive to possess. It should be our daily mission to live a life of integrity and to be empathetic. Empathy and compassion go a long way. Being disciplined, determined and consistent you are sure to find success following. Continuing her mission to inspire, Natacshia recently enrolled as a volunteer peer counselor for NYC 24hr Suicide Prevention Hotline. Where she will be providing crisis response and emotional support services to people who are in distress and suicidal. In all, these are more than past contributions to society but instead, a reflection of who Natacshia truly is, resilient a humanitarian and unstoppable.

www.ingramcontent.com/pod-product-compliance
Lightning Source LLC
Chambersburg PA
CBHW051438290426
44109CB00016B/1612